Cataraqui United Church Cemetary 3

The Grave Whisperer

Angeline Gallant

Published by Angeline Gallant, 2022.

CATARAQUI UNITED CHURCH CEMETARY 3

First edition. October 20, 2022.

ISBN: 979-8215268315

Written by Angeline Gallant.

Also by Angeline Gallant

Calling Her Heart
Whisper of the Heart
No Turning Back
Forsake Me Not
Hear My Cry

Keeper Of Secrets
A Lady's Secret

Midnight's Awakening
Heart of the Storm
Walking Through The Storm

Secrets of the Underworld
Deklan's Dragons

Tell My Story Collection

Tell My Story: England 1852

The Grave Whisperer
Wedding Bells in Kingston, Ontario, Canada 1923
St. Paul's Anglican Churchyard Kingston, Ontario, Canada A-B
St. Paul's Anglican Churchyard, Kingston, Ontario, Canada C - D
St. Paul's Anglican Churchyard, Kingston, Ontario, Canada G - H
St. Paul's Anglican Churchyard, Kingston, Ontario, Canada J - N
St. Paul's Anglican Churchyard, Kingston, Ontario, Canada O - R
St. Paul's Anglican Churchyard, Kingston, Ontario, Canada S - T
St. Paul's Anglican Churchyard, Kingston, Ontario T - Z
Small Graveyards & Burial Grounds: Kingston, Ontario, Canada
Cataraqui United Church Cemetery 1
Cataraqui United Church Cemetery 2
Cataraqui United Church Cemetary 3

The Wolf Whisperer Series
The Cry of the Wolf
Captured Heart
Journey of the Heart
Fate's Legacy
Wolf Whisperer volumes 1 & 2
Endless White

Standalone
Winds of Change vol 1-3

Table of Contents

ELIZABETH JANE CHEESEMAN[1]

Elizabeth was born on April 4, 1944.
She passed away a month later on March 23, 1944.

AMELIA (ANNING) CHOWN[2]

Amelia was born in England in 1828.

She was four years old when she immigrated to Canada in 1832.

Amelia was five years old when The Factory Act was passed in 1833.

She was 15 years old when A Christmas Carol was published in 1843.

Amelia was 22 years old when she married her sister's husband, Edwin Thorn Chown, on February 28, 1850. Her sister had passed away after giving birth.

She was 26 years old when her daughter, Elizabeth Anning, passed away on December 8, 1854. Her son, Herbert Henry, passed away ten days later on December 18th.

Amelia was 36 years old when her son, Herbert James, passed away in 1864.

She was 39 years old when Ontario was founded on July 1, 1867.

Amelia was 43 years old when British Columbia joined the confederation in 1871.

She was 52 years old when school attendance became mandatory for children in 1880.

Amelia was 76 years old when her husband passed away in 1803.

She was 78 years old when she passed away on May 28, 1806.

EDWIN THORN CHOWN[3]

Edwin was born in England in 1821.

He was 11 years old when his sister, Elizabeth Sarah, passed away in 1832.

Edwin was 21 years old when "A Christmas Carol" was first published in 1843.

He was 24 years old when he married Harriet Anning on December 9, 1845.

Edwin was 27 years old when his mother passed away in 1849. His wife and six-day-old son, Herbert, passed away on April 13, 1849.

He was 29 years old when he married Harriet's younger sister, Amelia, on February 28, 1850.

Edwin was 33 years old when his three-year-old daughter, Elizabeth Anning, passed away on December 8, 1854. Her two-year-old brother, Herbert Henry, passed away ten days later on December 18th.

He was 43 years old when his one-year-old son, Herbert James, passed away on August 8, 1864.

Edwin was 45 years old when Ontario was founded on July 1, 1867. He was 46 years old when his brother, Samuel, passed away on September 3rd.

He was 52 years old when his sister, Emma, passed away in 1873.

Edwin was 54 years old when his father passed away in 1875.

He was 61 years old when the mining boom in northern Ontario began in 1883.

Edwin was 77 years old when his brother, Arthur, passed away in 1898.

He was 78 years old when his brother, Lewis Thorn, passed away in 1899.

Edwin was 80 years old when his sister, Sarah, passed away in 1901.

He was 81 years old when his sister, Mahala passed away in 1902.

Edwin was 82 years old when he passed away on December 14, 1903. He was Methodist and a merchant.

REV. EDWIN ANNING CHOWN[4]

Edwin was born on October 16, 1846 in Kingston, Ontario. He was two years old when his mother and brother, Herbert, passed away in 1849.

Edwin was 20 years old when Ontario was founded on July 1, 1867.

He was 27 years old when he married Mary Richardson on November 6, 1873 in Kingston.

Edwin was 34 years old and a Methodist pastor in 1881. He was living in West Flamborough, Ontario.

He was 36 years old when the mining boom in northern Ontario began in 1883.

Edwin was 43 years old when the Women's Suffrage movement began in 1890.

He was 54 years old in 1901 and living in York, Ontario.

Edwin was 57 years old when his father passed away in 1903.

He was 64 years old when he immigrated to New York in November 1910.

Edwin was 66 years old when his daughter, Susannah Amelia, passed away in 1913.

He was 81 years old when his wife passed away in 1927. He passed away in 1928 and is buried in Kingston.

MARY (RICHARDSON) CHOWN[5]

Mary was born in Kingston, Ontario in 1846. She was Irish.

She was two years old when her mother passed away in 1848.

Mary was 21 years old when Ontario was founded on July 1, 1867.

She was 25 years old when British Columbia joined the confederation in 1871.

Mary was 27 years old when she married Rev. Edwin Anning Chown on November 6, 1873.

She was 35 years old and Methodist while living in West Flamborough, Ontario in 1881.

Mary was 37 years old when the mining boom in northern Ontario began in 1883.

She was 60 years old when Ontario Hydro was established in 1906.

Mary was 67 years old when her daughter, Susannah Amelia, passed away in 1913.

She was 81 years old when she passed away on November 24, 1927.

ROGER CHOWN[6]

Roger was born in England on September 8, 1794. He was christened on April 10, 1795 in Saint Mary Ottery, Devon, England.

Roger was 27 years old when he married Sarah Thorn on March 12, 1822 in Beer, Devon, England.

He was 28 years old when Rugby Football was invented in 1823.

Roger was 34 years old when his father passed away in 1828.

He was 37 years old when his daughter, Elizabeth Sarah, passed away in 1832.

Roger was 38 years old when the Factory Act was passed in 1833.

He was 40 years old when his mother passed away in 1835.

Roger was 47 years old when his brother, Henry, passed away in 1842.

He was 48 years old when "A Christmas Carol" was first published in 1843.

Roger was 54 years old when his wife passed away in 1849.

He was 66 years old when his sister, Sarah, passed away in 1861.

Roger was 72 years old when Ontario was founded on July 1, 1867.

He was 73 years old when his son, Samuel, passed away on September 3rd.

He was 75 years old when his brother, Richard, passed away in 1870.

Roger was 79 years old when his daughter, Emma, passed away in 1873.

He was 80 years old when he passed away on April 18, 1875.

SAMUEL CHOWN[7]

Samuel was born in England on December 27, 1825.

He was six years old when his sister, Elizabeth Sarah, passed away in 1832.

Samuel was seven years old when the Factory Act was passed in 1833.

He was 17 years old when "A Christmas Carol" was first published in 1843.

Samuel was 20 years old when he married Sarah Gardiner in 1846.

He was 22 years old when his daughter, Sarah, passed away in 1848.

Samuel was 23 years old when his mother passed away in 1849.

He was 41 years old when Ontario was founded on July 1, 1867. Samuel passed away on September 3rd.

SARAH (THORN) CHOWN[8]

Sarah was born in England on February 5, 1794.

She was six years old when the Act of Union was passed in 1801.

Sarah was 20 years old when Napoleon Bonaparte was defeated in 1815.

She was 27 years old when she gave birth to her first child, Edwin Thorn, on February 24, 1821. Sarah married his father, Roger Chown, the following year on March 12, 1822.

Sarah was 28 years old when Rugby Football was invented in 1823.

She was 38 years old when her daughter, Elizabeth Sarah, passed away in 1832.

Sarah was 48 years old when "A Christmas Carol" was first published in 1843.

She was 55 years old when she passed away on April 29, 1849.

SUSANNA AMELIA "SUSIE" CHOWN[9]

Susanna was born on November 28, 1874.

She was six years old and living in West Flamborough, Ontario in 1881.

Susie was eight years old when the mining boom in northern Ontario began in 1883.

She was 26 years old and Methodist, living in York, Ontario in 1901.

Susie was 38 years old when she passed away on September 28, 1913.

HANNAH CAROLINE (POWLEY) CLANCEY[10]

Hannah was born on October 31, 1833.

She was seven years old when her sister, Nancy, passed away in 1841.

Hannah was 29 years old when her sister, Mary, passed away on December 3, 1862.

She was 29 years old when she passed away on March 12, 1863.

ALICE JANE "ALLIE" (NICHOLSON) CLARK[11]

Allie was born on December 4, 1834. She was German.

She was 22 years old when she married Lewis Stover Clark in Ernestown in 1857.

Allie was 26 years old when her brother, Henry, passed away in 1861.

She was 32 years old when Ontario was founded on July 1, 1867.

Allie was Methodist.

She was 34 years old when her father passed away in 1869 and 35 years old when her mother passed away in 1870.

Allie was 48 years old when the mining boom in northern Ontario began in 1883.

She was 51 years old when the Statue of Liberty was dedicated in 1886.

Allie was 53 years old when her brother, Chester, passed away in 1888.

She was 59 years old when her son, Henry, passed away in 1893.

Allie was 65 years old when her daughter, Arvilla Philetta, passed away in 1900.

In 1901 she was 66 years old and living in Lennox, Ontario. Her niece and two granddaughters lived with Allie and her husband along with several "inmates."

She was 71 years old when Ontario Hydro was established in 1906.

Allie was 75 years old when her husband passed away in 1910.

She was 78 years old when the Central Banking System was established in 1913.

Allie was 79 years old when her sister, Margaret, passed away in 1914.

She was 80 years old when she passed away on September 8, 1915.

CHARLES SMITH CLARK[12]

Charles was born in 1825.

He was 26 years old when he married Martha Moores in Ernestown in 1852.

Charles was 29 years old when his sister, Jemima, passed away in 1855.

He was 38 years old when his father passed away in 1864.

Charles was 47 years old when his brother, Thomas Dyer, passed away in 1873.

He was 50 years old when his brother, Matthew Wright, passed away in 1876.

Charles was 52 years old when his brother, Peter Edward, passed away in 1878.

He was 57 years old when the mining boom in northern Ontario began in 1883.

Charles was 64 years old when his brother, Nathan John, passed away in 1889.

He was 65 years old when he passed away on March 6, 1891. Charles was a Methodist farmer.

GEORGE F. CLARK[13]

George was born in 1860.

He was seven years old when Ontario was founded on July 1, 1867.

George was 11 years old when British Columbia joined the confederation in 1871.

He was 23 years old when the mining boom in northern Ontario took place in 1883.

George was 26 years old when he married on January 27, 1886 in Collins Bay, Ontario.

He was 31 years old when his father passed away in 1891.

George was 33 years old when his sister, Caroline, passed away in 1893.

He was 46 years old when Ontario Hydro was established in 1906.

George was 83 years old when he passed away in 1943.

EDWIN HAROLD "HAROLD" RANKIN CLARK[14]

Harold was born on June 18, 1899 in Kingston, Ontario.

He was six years old when Ontario Hydro was established in 1906.

Harold was 34 years old when the Dionne Quintuplets were born in 1934.

He was 43 years old when his father passed away in 1943.

Harold was 49 years old when his mother passed away in 1949.

He was 73 years old when he passed away in 1973.

HARRIET ALBERTA (GUESS) CLARK[15]

Harriet was born in Portland, Ontario in December 1905.

She was ten years old when her brother, Barnabas Secord, passed away in 1916.

Harriet was 26 years old when her mother passed away in 1932.

She was 28 years old when the Dionne Quintuplets were born in 1934.

Harriet was 67 years old when her husband, Edwin Harold Rankin Clark, passed away in 1973.

She was 69 years old when she passed away in 1975.

MINERVA HELENA (RANKIN) CLARK[16]

Minerva was born in Kingston on April 16, 1868.

She was two years old when British Columbia joined the confederation in 1871.

Minerva was 14 years old when the mining boom in northern Ontario began in 1883.

She was 29 years old when she married George F. Clark in 1898.

Minerva was 35 years old when her father passed away in 1903.

She was 37 years old when Ontario Hydro was founded in 1906.

Minerva was 74 years old when her husband, George Franklin Clark, passed away in 1943.

She was 80 years old when she passed away in 1949.

HENRY N. CLARK[17]

Henry was born on December 23, 1865.

He was a year old when Ontario was founded on July 1, 1867.

Henry was 17 years old when the mining boom in northern Ontario began in 1883.

He was 24 years old when the Women's Suffrage movement began in 1890.

Henry was 27 years old when he passed away on November 30, 1893.

JANE M. (ATKINSON) CLARK[18]

Jane passed away on July 24, 1854.

JOHN NANTON "TONY" CLARK[19]

John was born on August 2, 1931 in Victoria, British Columbia.

He was 50 years old when the Canada Act was passed in 1982.

John was 74 years old when the Ontario Terrorism plot was foiled in 2006.

He was 88 years old when he passed away on February 25, 2020.

LEWIS STOVER CLARK[20]

Lewis was born in Ernestown, Addington, Upper Canada, British Colonial America on September 4, 1836.

He was 18 years old when his sister, Jemima, passed away in 1855.

Lewis was 20 years old when he married Alice Jane Nicholson in Ernestown in 1857.

He was 27 years old when his father passed away in 1864.

Lewis was 36 years old when his brother, Thomas Dyer, passed away in 1873.

He was 39 years old when his brother, Matthew Wright, passed away in 1876.

Lewis was 41 years old when his brother, Peter Edward, passed away in 1878.

He was 46 years old when the mining boom in northern Ontario took place in 1883.

Lewis was 53 years old when his brother, Nathan John, passed away in 1889.

He was 54 years old when his brother, Charles Smith, passed away in 1891.

Lewis was 57 years old when his son, Henry, passed away in 1893.

He was 63 years old when his daughter, Arvilla Philetta, passed away in 1900.

Lewis was 64 years old when his sister, Peregrine Maitland, passed away in 1901.

He was 69 years old when Ontario Hydro was established in 1906.

Lewis was 73 years old when the Mann Act was passed in 1910. His brother, John Colborne, passed away on April 7th. Lewis passed away a few months later on August 10th in Napanee, Ontario. He is buried in Kingston.

MARTHA (NICHOLSON) CLARK[21]

Martha was born in Ernestown, Upper Canada, on August 30, 1830.

She was 36 years old when Ontario was founded on July 1, 1867.

Martha was 40 years old when British Columbia joined the confederation in 1871.

She was 82 years old when she passed away on January 9, 1913 in Kingston, Ontario.

MARTHA (MOOERS) CLARK[22]

Martha was born in Upper Canada in 1830.

She was three years old when her sister, Margaret, passed away in 1833.

Martha was seven years old when her brother, Samuel, passed away in 1838.

She was 33 years old when her father passed away in 1863.

Martha was 36 years old when Ontario was founded on July 1, 1867.

She was 48 years old when her mother passed away in 1878.

Martha was 51 years old when the Chinese Exclusion Act was passed in 1882.

She was 54 years old when she passed away on November 25, 1884.

ROBERT CLARK[23]

Robert passed away on September 6, 1867 in Kingston, Frontenac, Canada West.

WILLIAM JACOB CLARK[24]

William was born in Ernestown, Upper Canada in 1827.

He was 28 years old when his sister, Jemima, passed away in 1855.

William was 37 years old when his father passed away in 1864.

He was 46 years old when his brother, Thomas Dyer, passed away in 1873.

William was 49 years old when his brother, Matthew Wright, passed away in 1876.

He was 51 years old when his brother, Peter Edward, passed away in 1878.

William was 56 years old when the mining boom in northern Ontario began in 1883.

He was 62 years old when his brother, Nathan John, passed away in 1889.

William was 64 years old when his brother, Charles Smith, passed away in 1891.

He was 73 years old when he passed away on July 1, 1900 in Kingston, Ontario where he is buried.

AGNES MARIA "DELLA" (LEHEUP) COGLON[25]

DELLA WAS BORN IN PITTSBURGH, Ontario on December 21, 1872.

She was 10 years old when the mining boom in northern Ontario began in 1883.

Della was 20 years old when her sister, Margorie, passed away in 1893.

She was 21 years old when her sister, Margret May, passed away on December 27, 1893.

Della was 28 years old when her sister, Mary Annie Louise, passed away in 1901.

She was 30 years old when her father passed away in 1903.

Della was 33 years old when Ontario Hydro was established in 1906.

She was 46 years old when her mother passed away in 1919.

Della was 60 years old when she passed away on August 22, 1933.

ISAAC ISRAEL SMITH COGLON[26]

Isaac was born in Kingston on August 15, 1847. He was Irish.

He was 27 years old when he married Mary Cecilia Oster on October 20, 1874 in Storrington, Ontario. His father passed away on May 18, 1875.

Isaac was 34 years old when the Chinese Exclusion Act was passed in 1882.

He was 57 years old when his mother passed away in 1904.

Isaac was 58 years old when his wife passed away in 1906.

He was 62 years old when the Mann Act was passed in 1910. Isaac married Lydia Holland on January 10th in Kingston, Ontario. She was 44 years old.

In 1911 he was 63 years old and Methodist. Isaac was living in Medicine Hat, Alberta.

By 1916 he was living in Lethbridge, Alberta.

He was 71 years old when his sister, Louisa Jane, passed away in 1919.

Isaac was 72 years old when his son, Morris Franklin, passed away in 1920.

He was 76 years old when his sister, Sarah, passed away in 1923.

Isaac was 77 years old when his sister, Elizabeth Agnes, passed away in 1924.

He was 78 years old when he passed away in Ontario on April 3, 1926.

MARY CECELIA (ORSTER) COGLON[27]

ary was born on January 11, 1851. She was German. Mary was living in Storrington, Ontario in 1851.

She was 10 years old when her brother, Ira, passed away in 1862.

Mary was 19 years old when British Columbia joined the confederation in 1871.

She was 23 years old when she married Isaac Isreal Smith Coglon on October 20, 1874 in Storrington, Ontario.

Mary was 31 years old when the mining boom in northern Ontario began in 1883.

She was 42 years old when her brother, Isaiah, passed away in 1893.

Mary was 49 years old when her mother passed away on March 16, 1900. Her father passed away a few months later on June 15th.

In 1901 she was 50 years old and living in Lennox, Ontario. Mary was Methodist.

She was 55 years old when Ontario Hydro was established in 1906. Her sister, Candace Gertrude, passed away the same year. Mary passed away on June 27th.

MORRIS FRANKLIN COGLON M.D. [28]

Morris was born in Kingston, Ontario on April 18, 1880. He was two years old when the mining boom in northern Ontario began in 1883.

Morris was 25 years old when Ontario Hydro was established in 1906. His mother passed away on June 27th when Morris was 26 years old.

He was 35 years old when he married Della Leheup on August 18, 1915 in Kingston, Ontario.

Morris was 36 years old when his infant daughter, Edna Reta, passed away in 1916

He was 39 years old and a doctor when he passed away on February 19, 1920 in Hamilton, Ontario. Morris is buried in Kingston. He was married to Della.

FLORENCE MAPLE (WARE) CONNOLLY[29]

Florence was born in Ottawa, Ontario in 1906, the same year that Ontario Hydro was established.

She was 64 years old when she passed away on August 25, 1970.

HAROLD JOHN "HARRY" CONNOLLY[30]

Harry was born in London, England in 1903.

He was 53 years old when Queen Elizabeth was crowned in 1953.

Harry was 60 years old when he passed away in 1963.

HELEN GLADYS COPLEY[31]

Helen was eight months old when she passed away in September 1897.

THOMAS EDWIN COPLEY[32]

Thomas was born in November 1909.

He was only a month old when he passed away on December 22, 1909.

JOHN CORDUKES[33]

John was born in York, Yorkshire England on April 6, 1798. He was christened on April 29th.

He was 33 years old when he married Sarah Jane Thomas Cook on April 24, 1831 in Holtby, York, England.

John was 38 years old when his brother, Thomas, passed away in 1837.

He was 44 years old when "A Christmas Carol" was published in 1843. His sister, Mary Ann Preston, passed away the same year.

John was 70 years old when his sister, Elisabeth, passed away in 1869.

He was 72 years old when British Columbia joined the confederation in 1871. Both his wife and daughter, Jane, passed away that year.

John was 73 years old when he passed away three months after his wife's death on October 19, 1871. He was Methodist.

JOHN COUSINEAU[34]

John passed away in 2008.

MARGARET (CRAIG) THOMPSON[35]

Margaret was born in 1789.
She was 58 years old when she passed away in 1847.

ALICE MARY (BARRY) CRAMER[36]

Alice was born on July 6, 1900 in Frontenac, Ontario. She was Irish. She was five years old when Ontario Hydro was established in 1906.

Alice was 17 years old when her brother, Phillip Stewart, passed away in 1918.

She was 20 years old when she married Fenwick George Cramer in Kingston, Ontario in 1920.

Alice was 33 years old when the Dionne Quintuplets were born in 1934.

She was 56 years old when her husband passed away in 1957.

Alice was 81 years old when the Canada Act was passed in 1982.

She was 92 years old when she passed away in 1992.

FENWICK GEORGE CRAMER[37]

Fenwick was born in Kingston, Ontario on November 15, 1875. He was Dutch.

He was seven years old when the mining boom in northern Ontario began in 1883.

Fenwick was 30 years old when Ontario Hydro was established in 1906.

He was 44 years old when he married Alice Mary Barry in 1920.

Fenwick was 68 years old when his brother, Cromwell Dawson, passed away in 1944.

He was 81 years old when he passed away on January 2, 1957. Fenwick was Methodist.

EMMA (WALKER) CRAMER[38]

Emma was born in 1861.

She was six years old when Ontario was founded on July 1, 1867.

Emma was 10 years old when British Columbia joined the confederation in 1871.

She was 80 years old when she passed away in 1941.

JOSEPH CRAMER[39]

Joseph was born in 1853. He was Dutch.

He was 14 years old when Ontario was founded on July 1, 1867.

Joseph was 18 years old when British Columbia joined the confederation in 1871.

He was 81 years old when he passed away in 1934.

ROSA MAUD CRAMER[40]

Rosa was born on February 24, 1886 in Kingston. She was Dutch. She was 19 years old when Ontario Hydro was established in 1906.

Rosa was 47 years old when her father passed away in 1934.

She was 53 years old when she passed away in 1940.

ABRAHAM CREMER[41]

Abraham passed away on February 20, 1841 and is buried in Kingston, Ontario.

CATHERINE CRESSALL[42]

Catherine passed away on March 20, 1856.

EDWARD CRESSALL[43]

Edward was 20 years old when he passed away on November 30, 1855. He is buried with his mother, Catherine.

LUCY E. (LAKE) CROWN[44]

Lucy was born on October 31, 1884.

She was seven years old when the women's suffrage movement began in 1890.

Lucy was 12 years old when her sister, Edith Boothe, passed away in 1895.

She was 23 years old when Ontario Hydro was established in 1906.

Lucy was 25 years old when she married Albert Crown in New Jersey in 1908.

She was 27 years old when the Mann Act was passed in 1910.

Lucy was 39 years old when she passed away on July 27, 1922 in Philadelphia. She is buried in Kingston, Ontario.

PVT. JAMES LEWIS GILBERT DAFOE[45]

James was born on March 15, 1887 in Kaladar, Ontario.

He was 18 years old when Ontario Hydro was established in 1906.

James was 36 years old when he married Margaret Matilda on March 23, 1923 in Kingston, Ontario. His father passed away on August 29th.

He was 46 years old when the Dionne Quintuplets were born in 1934.

James was 65 years old when he passed away on January 13, 1953.

JAMES MITCHELL DAFOE[46]

James was born in Kaladar, Ontario on May 24, 1865. He was Scottish/German/French.

He was a year old when Ontario was founded on July 1, 1867.

James was five years old when British Columbia joined the confederation in 1871.

He was 21 years old when he married Mary Matilda on May 27, 1886 in Flinton, Ontario.

James was 40 years old when Ontario Hydro was established in 1906.

He was 45 years old when his daughter, Catherine Pearl, passed away in 1911.

James was 46 years old when his mother passed away in 1912.

He was Methodist.

James was 56 years old when he married Ida in Deseronto, Ontario on February 13, 1922. She was 37 years old.

James was 58 years old when he passed away on August 29, 1923 in Adolphustown, Ontario. He was buried in Kingston on August 31st.

CHARLOTTE JANE DALY[47]

Charlotte was born in 1830.

She was 16 years old when her father passed away in 1846. Charlotte was 23 years old when she passed away in 1853.

GEORGE WELLINGTON DALY[48]

George was born in 1837.

He was nine years old when his father passed away in 1846.

George was 16 years old when his sister, Charlotte Jane, passed away in 1853.

He was 30 years old when he passed away in 1867.

JOHN DALY[49]

John was born in 1823.

He was 23 years old when his father passed away in 1846.

John was 30 years old when his sister, Charlotte Jane, passed away in 1853.

He was 44 years old when Ontario was founded on July 1, 1867. His brother, George Wellington, passed away that year.

John was 60 years old when his mother passed away in 1883.

He was 77 years old when he passed away in 1900.

JUSTUS WALLBRIDGE DALY[50]

Justus was born in Kingston, Ontario in 1823. He was Irish.

He was seven years old when his father passed away in 1846.

Justus was 14 years old when his sister, Charlotte Jane, passed away in 1853.

He was 28 years old when his brother, George Wellington, passed away in 1867.

Justus was 29 years old when he married Eliza Ann on October 26, 1868. He was Methodist and a farmer.

He was 44 years old when his mother passed away in 1883.

Justus was 60 years old when his brother, John, passed away in 1900.

He was 66 years old when Ontario Hydro was established in 1906.

Justus was 74 years old when his brother, James, passed away in 1913.

He was 75 years old when he passed away on April 14, 1915.

LEWIS LUDOWICK DALY[51]

Lewis was born in 1794.

He was 38 years old when his father passed away in 1832.

Lewis was 43 years old when his sisters, Catherine and Anna, passed away in 1837.

He was 45 years old when his mother passed away in 1839.

Lewis was 52 years old when he passed away in 1846.

[1] https://www.wikitree.com/genealogy/Cheeseman-Family-Tree-1042

[2] https://www.wikitree.com/genealogy/Anning-Family-Tree-40

[3] https://www.wikitree.com/genealogy/Chown-Family-Tree-148

[4] https://www.wikitree.com/genealogy/Chown-Family-Tree-155

[5] https://www.wikitree.com/genealogy/Richardson-Family-Tree-20744

[6] https://www.wikitree.com/genealogy/Chown-Family-Tree-150

[7] https://www.wikitree.com/genealogy/Chown-Family-Tree-335

[8] https://www.wikitree.com/genealogy/Thorn-Family-Tree-1010

[9] https://www.wikitree.com/genealogy/Chown-Family-Tree-336

[10] https://www.wikitree.com/genealogy/Powley-Family-Tree-446

[11] https://www.wikitree.com/genealogy/Nicholson-Family-Tree-10737

[12] https://www.wikitree.com/genealogy/Clark-Family-Tree-76520

[13] https://www.wikitree.com/genealogy/Clark-Family-Tree-76521

[14] https://www.wikitree.com/genealogy/Clark-Family-Tree-76522

[15] https://www.wikitree.com/genealogy/Guess-Family-Tree-611

[16] https://www.wikitree.com/genealogy/Rankin-Family-Tree-4977

[17] https://www.wikitree.com/genealogy/Clark-Family-Tree-76523

[18] https://www.wikitree.com/genealogy/Atkinson-Family-Tree-12989

[19] https://www.wikitree.com/genealogy/Clark-Family-Tree-76560

[20] https://www.wikitree.com/genealogy/Clark-Family-Tree-76562

[21] https://www.wikitree.com/genealogy/Nicholson-Family-Tree-10742

[22] https://www.wikitree.com/genealogy/Mooers-Family-Tree-352

[23] https://www.wikitree.com/genealogy/Clark-Family-Tree-76591

[24] https://www.wikitree.com/genealogy/Clark-Family-Tree-76600

[25] https://www.wikitree.com/genealogy/Leheup-Family-Tree-10

[26] https://www.wikitree.com/genealogy/Coglon-Family-Tree-2

[27] https://www.wikitree.com/genealogy/Orser-Family-Tree-527

[28] https://www.wikitree.com/genealogy/Coglon-Family-Tree-3

[29] https://www.wikitree.com/genealogy/Ware-Family-Tree-5600

[30] https://www.wikitree.com/genealogy/Connolly-Family-Tree-3565

[31] https://www.wikitree.com/genealogy/Copley-Family-Tree-1940

[32] https://www.wikitree.com/genealogy/Copley-Family-Tree-1941

[33] https://www.wikitree.com/genealogy/Cordukes-Family-Tree-60

[34] https://www.wikitree.com/genealogy/Cousineau-Family-Tree-617

[35] https://www.wikitree.com/genealogy/Craig-Family-Tree-14449

[36] https://www.wikitree.com/genealogy/Barry-Family-Tree-6196

[37] https://www.wikitree.com/genealogy/Cramer-Family-Tree-4104

[38] https://www.wikitree.com/genealogy/Walker-Family-Tree-60600

[39] https://www.wikitree.com/genealogy/Cramer-Family-Tree-4120

[40] https://www.wikitree.com/genealogy/Cramer-Family-Tree-4121

[41] https://www.wikitree.com/genealogy/Creamer-Family-Tree-338

[42] https://www.wikitree.com/genealogy/Cressall-Family-Tree-18

[43] https://www.wikitree.com/genealogy/Cressall-Family-Tree-19

[44] https://www.wikitree.com/genealogy/Lake-Family-Tree-6017

[45] https://www.wikitree.com/genealogy/Dafoe-Family-Tree-339

[46] https://www.wikitree.com/genealogy/Dafoe-Family-Tree-342

[47] https://www.wikitree.com/genealogy/Daly-Family-Tree-4143

[48] https://www.wikitree.com/genealogy/Daly-Family-Tree-4144

[49] https://www.wikitree.com/genealogy/Daly-Family-Tree-4145

[50] https://www.wikitree.com/genealogy/Daly-Family-Tree-4146

[51] https://www.wikitree.com/genealogy/Daly-Family-Tree-4147

Don't miss out!

Visit the website below and you can sign up to receive emails whenever Angeline Gallant publishes a new book. There's no charge and no obligation.

https://books2read.com/r/B-A-QGSI-DVDCC

BOOKS 2 READ

Connecting independent readers to independent writers.

Also by Angeline Gallant

Calling Her Heart
Whisper of the Heart
No Turning Back
Forsake Me Not
Hear My Cry

Keeper Of Secrets
A Lady's Secret

Midnight's Awakening
Heart of the Storm
Walking Through The Storm

Secrets of the Underworld
Deklan's Dragons

Tell My Story Collection

Watch for more at https://www.goodreads.com/author/show/19703964.Angeline_Gallant.

www.ingramcontent.com/pod-product-compliance
Lightning Source LLC
Chambersburg PA
CBHW052228150726
48002CB00003B/1320